T0147168

A
TRUE LOVE STORY
PRECIOUS

PAUL CROSS

WESTBOW
PRESS®
A DIVISION OF THOMAS NELSON
& ZONDERVAN

WestBow Press books may be ordered through booksellers or by contacting:

WestBow Press
A Division of Thomas Nelson & Zondervan
1663 Liberty Drive
Bloomington, IN 47403
www.westbowpress.com
1 (866) 928-1240

ISBN: 978-1-9736-7670-6 (sc)
ISBN: 978-1-9736-7669-0 (e)

Print information available on the last page.

WestBow Press rev. date: 10/7/2019

*This writing is a synopsis of a story that,
if written in its entirety,
would require more energy and effort
than I am capable of giving at this stage of my life.*

Love is not Love until it is given away.

*So if this short, true Love Story is successful
in touching your mind and/or your heart,
please tell those whom you love and who love you
about the book.*

*It will cost you nothing,
but the rewards may last a lifetime.*

We Thank You! We Love You!!!

Paul Cross

Contents

Acknowledgement

As always, Lord Jesus, You knew that in the spring of 2018 when Precious was in her fourth month of hospice care, and the cancer was spreading throughout her body, that I was planning a birthday gift to present to her on August 22nd.

It would be a short story reminding her of our first meeting and our first date as teenagers.

Later, You gave me the inspiration to expand the story and prepare it for publication. I was approaching my ninety-fourth year of life and would need someone to help me who was familiar with the publishing business and was internet savvy.

This lady who was cleaning our quarters had written a novel for publication and circulation and was presently writing another. This lady volunteered to help produce this book.

After Precious had passed away the only way I could relieve my heartache was to write about our life together. This book would tell that story. This lady volunteered her time and expertise.

Writing this was an effective temporary catharsis for my overwhelming grief caused by the passing of my Precious.

I am very Thankful to You Lord Jesus for bringing this lady, Cate Radebaugh, into our lives.

Preface

When I met them in the spring of 2018, Paul Cross was ninety-three and his beloved wife Betty was ninety-two and moving as slowly as she could toward the end of her life. I had come to help with a few small household tasks, but soon found myself engaged in a lively, loving conversation I came to know was typical of them. We discovered - in a 'what are the odds?' kind of way - that we had places and people in common from years ago. By the time I left that day, I felt as though we'd known each other for decades. The Crosses had that effect on people.

Betty Cross loved her life here with Paul and stayed with him as long as she could. She knew, as he knows, that their love transcends death. Theirs is and will be forever A True Love Story.

Cate Radebaugh

Dear Sweet Jesus, my Lord and my God,
I will never be able to adequately
Praise and Thank You enough
for all that You have given me.
At the age of fifteen,
You knew that I would soon be in
desperate need for someone in my life.
As an orphan and soon to be homeless,
You brought this "angel" into my life.

1

A Gift from Heaven

In the late spring of 1941, the high schools in the county were having their Annual Track and Field Day Competition at Annapolis High School where I was a student in my sophomore year. Bill Butler, a classmate of mine, and I decided to go and watch some of the girls' races.

We no sooner arrived when the sixty yard dash began. Immediately my eyes became fixed on a skinny little girl who was running "like the wind." She had the most beautiful face I had ever seen.

Bill said to me, "She can really run."

I replied, "She sure can. But I can catch her."

The race ended and she disappeared into her

group of other track team members who were from the Glen Burnie High School. She was gone, but "That Face" had been instantly and permanently etched into my memory.

2

The Meeting

A few weeks later on a Sunday after attending church services, the aunt with whom I was living at that time said to me, "I am driving up to Ferndale today to visit a lady friend that attended nursing school with me. Would you like to ride along? By the way, she has a teenage daughter who is near your age."

I thought about what she said for a few seconds, then I surprised myself by replying, "Yes, I will ride along with you."

I knew at that time that Aunt Helen was definitely one of the worst drivers in the world. I could only surmise that she wanted me to ride along so I would be of assistance if car problems developed while traveling.

After arriving at our destination and the introductions, I learned that the daughter of her friend, Mabel Unger, was out with friends and she would soon be home. I sat in the sunroom at the front of the home and was reading the Sunday newspaper.

Twenty minutes later, I heard excited young voices outdoors at the front of the home. Then the sound of feet bounding up the steps, the front door flew open, and there it was, "That Face!"

Immediately, excitedly, I said, "Hi!" as this blur passed by me with a barely audible "Hi."

It was her!! I could not believe what had just happened! (Oh God, You know, Lord Jesus, how unworthy I am.)

She informed her mother (Mabel) that Betty Jane and Rosetta were going to the movies and she would like to go with them. Her mother approved (I did not know at that time that 99.9 percent of her requests were granted by her family. She had their complete confidence because she was so trustworthy.) We were then introduced by my aunt.

"Betty, this is Paul. Paul, this is Betty." (I thought, "Can life get any better than this?")

And then Betty's mother said, "Why don't you take Paul with you to the movies? Because Helen and I will be spending the remainder of the day together planning a trip."

(I thought, "This cannot be real, I must be dreaming.")

And then, reality set in.

I said to Aunt Helen, "You are driving home before dark, aren't you?"

(The thought of her driving at night on the Governor Richie Highway at speeds of twenty-five and thirty mph on a Sunday evening was a thought that could ruin my entire unreal day.)

She assured me that we would drive back before dark.

Then I said to Betty, "Shall we be on our way?"

On the way out of the home, I told Betty I had watched her as she ran at the recent Track and Field Day at Annapolis High School. (I had watched her running that day, Lord Jesus, and You were there.) I waited until that evening to tell Betty that I had been unable to stop thinking about her after watching her run at the races.

3

First Togetherness

As we rode the train the short distance to Glen Burnie, where the theater was located, Betty Jane and Rosetta sat on a seat facing Betty and I on the opposite seat. I watched Betty's face as the three of them talked mostly about the movie that was playing. I answered Betty Jane's and Rosetta's questions concerning myself while continuing to divert the conversation to their lives.

At the theater, I was thrilled having Betty sitting next to me. I kept watching her face as often as possible throughout the movie. About halfway through the movie, I gently placed my arm at the back of her seat at the top so that my arm lightly touched both of her shoulders. She was aware of my arm, but did not say anything when she looked at me and smiled softly.

After the movie, we all had a soda at the local drugstore and then rode the train back to Ferndale. Betty Jane and Rosetta said goodbye and Betty and I returned to her home.

Dinner was served to all. Most of the conversation at dinner was between Aunt Helen and Mabel. Our real togetherness began after dinner, when Betty and I went out on the back lawn and entered a well constructed, well-furnished gazebo.

4

Getting to Know You

We entered the gazebo and sat facing each other as we talked and talked. I wanted to know everything about her life: Her full name, her address, her phone number, everything. Did she like music? Yes! She bought a new 45 rpm record every week in Baltimore. What type of music? All types! Did she swim? Yes! She has a bike and enjoys riding with friends. Did she dance? Yes! Great! I like to dance. Betty spoke softly, clearly, and her very expressive eyes gleamed as she spoke. I could not stop looking into her eyes and watching her face.

Betty was baptized Roman Catholic! I was baptized Roman Catholic! She dearly loved her deceased paternal grandmother. I dearly loved my deceased maternal grandmother. At this point in our conversation, I became aware that something wonderful was happening to me and I did not want it to ever end. I could not stop looking at her face or listening to her voice.

More about her: She was fourteen years old and would be fifteen on August 22. Born August 22, 1926. I was born in 1925. Her full Christian name: Frances Elizabeth Cecilia Merrifield. Although she was known in Ferndale and Glen Burnie and in Baltimore and in high school as "Betty Unger." Her mother had married approximately two years earlier to a man by the name of Frederick Unger who had recently died.

Betty admired Fred and was very pleased at having him as her stepfather. He had owned his own business and was teaching Betty about the more cultured aspects of life.

Betty said that she loved her Aunt Hattie, who had come to live with her and her mother after Fred died. As a child, Betty had been reared mostly by her grandmother and Aunt Hattie. Aunt Hattie had and was presently teaching Betty many things about life and living. She was truly more like a mother to Betty than Betty's real mother.

Prior to living in Ferndale with her mother and Fred, her mother had enrolled Betty as a full-time, five days a week, student at St. Mildred's Academy for Girls in Laurel, Maryland. It was a Catholic boarding school for girls operated by the Pallottine Order of Teaching Nuns. Betty was happy there and had enjoyed the time she spent at the Academy. Three years total.

More information I garnered about Betty: her address: P.O. Box 51, Ferndale MD; her telephone number: Glen Burnie 309. She is a natural left-handed writer, but writes with her right hand also. She can write with both hands simultaneously in opposite directions. Like Leonardo da Vinci, she was born a natural "mirror" writer.

Her weekly allowance: $15.00. (At that time, 1941, the weekly salary of the average man with a family was $30-40.00.) Although Betty was very kind and generous by nature and very popular at school, I could not but think that perhaps that her "friends" at school wanted to keep "friendly" with her because of her allowance. The allowance of most students at that time was .50 - $1.00 per week.

As a fourteen-year-old girl, Betty was very well dressed and groomed. She frequented the beauty parlor weekly. She had well-kept, dark, naturally wavy shoulder length hair that smelled heavenly. (I had smelled her hair while placing my arm around her shoulders in the theater.) I asked her if it would be all right if I sat next to her on the small sofa where she was sitting. She said it would be all right. (Let me state that as a young teenager, I always acted very properly and politely when in the presence of females. I would never permit any of my male friends to be rude or crude when in the presence of females.)

We sat together. I held her hand in mine and we talked until it was time for me to leave. I asked her if it would be all right with her if I came to be with her the next Sunday.

She said, "Yes!!"

(And through it all, You were there with us, Sweet Jesus!!!)

5

Aunt Hattie

The following Sunday, I arrived at Betty's home at two o'clock in the afternoon. Her Aunt Hattie, a very attractive woman in her forties, met me at the door and invited me in. We introduced ourselves and I immediately liked her. She was soft-spoken and very welcoming. We entered the living room as Betty appeared. We said "hello." I told Betty that it was good seeing her again. The three of us sat and talked for a few hours. I asked about their family. Aunt Hattie was very informative and volunteered much.

Aunt Hattie is Betty's biological father's sister. Her mother was the grandmother that Betty had lived with during most of Betty's childhood. Many of the Merrifield family had lived together in a large country home during the Great Depression. Betty's mother lived in the nurse's quarters where she had trained to be a nurse. After her training, she continued to live in the quarters while a nurse at the hospital where she had trained. She did not live with the Merrifields as she had divorced Betty's father when Betty was nine years of age. Betty had lived at her grandmother's home along with her grandfather, father, Aunt Hattie who was also divorced, and two other brothers of Aunt Hattie.

Aunt Hattie was very talented. She loved music. She sang and played the piano, was a very good cook, graduated from nursing school, and was presently working as the chief seamstress at one of the largest department stores in Baltimore. When Betty was living with them, her grandmother, who was also a seamstress, made all of Betty's clothing.

Betty's father, Hobart R. Merrifield, was a builder. But he usually worked alone because of a severe hearing defect suffered from a childhood disease. Uncle Homer, the oldest brother, was a master plumber working in Washington DC.

Uncle Bill, the youngest brother, was a self-employed mechanic and a violinist. All of the brothers were excellent workers. Unfortunately, they all drank heavily every weekend, which upset her grandmother very much, although she reluctantly tolerated it.

Betty and Aunt Hattie then wanted to know about my background. I told them that I had become ill as a child before I had learned to walk. I was diagnosed with poliomyelitis, and my left leg was paralyzed, which prevented me from walking until I was almost five years of age. At four, almost five years of age, I became ill with scarlet fever. A few weeks later, when the scarlet fever was gone, the pain and paralysis in my leg was also gone. Then I learned to walk, which made my parents very happy, especially my mother. I told Betty and Aunt Hattie that not long after getting well, when I was five years old, my mother, whom I loved very dearly, died. Which left me devastated! I had spent every waking moment of my young life near or within hearing of my mother. It was soon after her death that my Lord Jesus came into my life in a very positive manner.

I told Betty and Aunt Hattie that I had three sisters, two older than myself and one younger. I had a deceased younger brother who had died in infancy. My father had remarried before I turned six years old. I had a very cruel stepmother.

My father died 16 November 1940. After the funeral, Uncle Lloyd, one of my father's brothers, took me to live with him and his wife, Helen, in Annapolis, MD. I had been living with them for seven months or so.

While we were talking, Aunt Hattie asked Betty and I to come sit in the breakfast nook part of the kitchen while she prepared dinner. Aunt Hattie served dinner in the dining room. Being a growing boy of fifteen, I ate heartily of the deliciously prepared meal. Lucky me! A very pleasant lady cooking and serving a deliciously prepared meal and sitting next to the prettiest girl I had ever met. Wow! Can it get any better than this???

After dinner, I asked them if they would join me in taking the Moonlight Cruise out of the Baltimore Harbor and down part of the Chesapeake Bay and back in port by midnight.

It would be a dinner/dance affair with full orchestra. Betty to be my date and Aunt Hattie as her chaperone. I would pay the entire cost for the three of us. Aunt Hattie said that she previously had taken the cruise and had an enjoyable evening. We all agreed it would be a nice way to spend an evening together. We scheduled to go the following Saturday evening. I was inwardly overjoyed at the prospect of holding this beautiful, very pleasant young girl in my arms while dancing. Saturday afternoon could not come fast enough for me.

I thanked both of them for an enjoyable afternoon and early evening together and we said our farewells.

6

From Sublime to Surreal

I arrived home in Annapolis that evening and noticed that there was no one at home. Both Uncle Lloyd and Aunt Helen were gone. Quite unusual. At nine o'clock in the evening, I went upstairs to go to bed. While preparing for bed, I heard my Uncle Lloyd coming up the stairs. He came into my room and I noticed that he appeared very drunk and he smelled of whiskey. I asked him if he was all right. He scowled at me and became very belligerent. I had not seen him as such before and was surprised at his behavior. I tried to avoid any confrontation. He spoke ill of and belittled my father and said that he had always wanted to punch my father in the face. Then he said he wanted to punch me in the face because I reminded him of my father. I was surprised and shocked, so I told him, "If it will make you feel any better in your mind, then go ahead and punch me." So he punched me once in the face. As the blood trickled down, I asked him if he felt any better. He looked at me with a strange look on his face and then he began to cry softly. Then I began to cry. Not because I was hurting, but because I was so disappointed with his behavior. He said that he was sorry and asked me to please forgive him, which I did. Then he went to his bedroom. He spent the following Monday and Tuesday in a bar down the street, but he avoided me.

Usually, my Uncle Lloyd was a very nice, soft spoken, courteous, compassionate gentleman. I had admired and loved him since my childhood, because of the many kindnesses he had shown me. I would not change my feelings for him because of this one unpleasant incident.

In years following, I traveled for visits with him after his wife, Aunt Helen, had abandoned him. He and I spent hours speaking with each other until his untimely, self-imposed death. I attended his funeral and military burial in the Arlington National Cemetery, honoring a man who had served his country with honor for thirty years. May our dear Lord Jesus grant him the peace of soul that he was unable to find while alive on this earth. Amen! Amen!!!

Late Wednesday, Aunt Helen came home. She said that she and I would have a very important talk after breakfast on Thursday morning.

7

Out You Go

Thursday morning, after breakfast, Aunt Helen told me that the previous November, when Uncle Lloyd had called while in Pennsylvania preparing for the funeral of my father, he had asked her if he could bring me home with him to live with them because none of us children wanted to remain living with our stepmother. Aunt Helen told him that she would approve only if he would promise her that he would stop his habit of "binge" drinking. He promised her that he would stop.

Well, being an alcoholic, he "fell off the wagon" after six months or so and started drinking again. She reminded him of his promise and told him that I could no longer live with them. She said that on the next Saturday, she and Mabel Unger would be leaving on a trip to Atlantic City, NJ, and that I must be gone from the home before her return the following Wednesday. I would need to find somewhere else to live! She was very factual, cold, and unrelenting. I Had To Go!!!

What Must I Do??? … Where Can I Go??? … Lord Jesus, please help me as You have always done in the past! Show me the way!!!

Immediately, I went to my room to think. The plan formed almost immediately and completely in my mind. I wrote a quick, short note to relatives in southwestern Pennsylvania saying that I would call them from the bus station in Brownsville when I arrived next Sunday afternoon. I mailed the letter on my way to the Old Oak Dairy Depot. I told the manager of the Depot that I would no longer work helping to deliver milk to customers. I went to the distributor's office of the Washington Post and gave up my newspaper route. Then I sold my bicycle to another carrier who was in the office. I went to the bus station and picked up a bus schedule for the Greyhound Bus Station in Washington, D.C. I went home and figured out the time it would take to get from home to the Greyhound Station in Washington in time to catch a bus to Pennsylvania. Then I went to the bar where Uncle Lloyd was sitting and asked him if he would be sober enough on Sunday morning to be able to drive me to the Greyhound Station in Washington. He assured me that he would and he said that he would pay for my ticket to any place that I desired to go. We shook hands on the plan and I went home.

All had been accomplished in one day. I felt very relieved and I owe it all to You, Sweet Jesus, for revealing the plan to me. I Thank You!! I Thank You!!! I had a total of $44.00 and a date with the nicest, prettiest girl in the world this coming Saturday evening. I would spend tomorrow planning and packing.

In the afternoon on the following Saturday, I rode the electric train to Ferndale. Aunt Helen rode along with me as she was to leave with Mabel Unger on their trip to Atlantic City. They were to leave soon after our arrival. After arriving with greetings and pleasantries, Aunt Helen and Betty's mother departed.

Betty, Aunt Hattie, and I talked for an hour or more and then they decided to get dressed for the evening. When they appeared all dressed, they both looked so charming. I complimented both of them. Their dresses and medium heeled shoes were perfect for our planned evening. I was wearing brown trousers, a shirt and tie, and a light tan sport coat. Betty was wearing a light summer dress that was a perfect fit. She was so beautiful, inwardly as well as outwardly. I felt so honored and thankful for having the privilege to escort an "angel."

8

The Moonlight Cruise

At the ship, an orchestra was playing as we were welcomed aboard. The ship was well appointed for a moonlight cruise. We were escorted to our table in the dining room, near a window where we had a nice view of the harbor.

Soon the ship weighed anchor and sailed out of the harbor. Before long, the waiter appeared with menus for dinner. We three chose beef with side dishes and salads. The dinner was well prepared and the service was excellent.

After dessert, we sat and talked while relaxing. I thought it would be an opportune time to tell them that I was being evicted and would be leaving to go to Pennsylvania the next day.

I told them that I did not know where or with

whom I would be living, but I was confident that our dear Lord Jesus would guide me to the place where I was to go. They both expressed their surprise and dismay. I assured them that I would be all right and that I was confident that someday we would all meet again. So let us forget about tomorrow and enjoy our evening. Saying that lightened the moment and we did not mention my leaving again until we returned to Betty's home. I danced with Betty often and some with Aunt Hattie. They were both smooth dancers.

Betty and I walked the deck together and we would stop at the rail to view the sky and bay along with the lights of the towns on shore as we traveled. We talked of things of mutual interest. Aunt Hattie permitted us to spend much time together without her being present. She was confident that our actions would be proper at all times, a trust that Betty and I welcomed and were grateful to have.

As the ship sailed back into the harbor, the orchestra started playing the song "Good Night, Sweetheart." We danced the last dance and I held her closer to me. I was thrilled and sad at the same time.

We returned to port and the three of us were very pleased with our evening spent together. I paid the bill for the three of us over Aunt Hattie's objections. I felt that the $33.00 that it cost was well spent for the most pleasant evening I had ever experienced. Besides, I still had $11.00 in my pocket. You could do much with $11.00 at that time. (Note: one dollar in 1941 is worth $17.28 in 2019. In 1941, $11.00 was like having $190.08 today.)

Back at the home of Betty, it was decided that I would sleep on the "daybed," then take the first train to Annapolis Sunday morning. Aunt Hattie and I hugged and said our goodbyes. Then she retired to her bedroom.

Betty and I sat together on the sofa. I told her how very much I enjoyed being with her, and that I hoped and prayed that someday we would be seeing each other again. She said that she hoped so, also. We were holding hands as we talked, so I asked her if she had ever been kissed by a boy. She replied no she had not. I asked her if it would be all right with her if I gave her her first kiss. She said yes. So I held her head with both hands and kissed her as softly and as gently as possible. I knew then that I would cherish that moment forever. And I have!

The next morning, we said goodbye at the train station. I promised Betty that we would see each other again.

Sometime! ... Somewhere!! ... Somehow!!!

9

World War II

On December 7, 1941, at dawn, the Japanese attacked and destroyed a portion of the Pacific Fleet of the United States Navy that was at anchor at Pearl Harbor, Hawaii.

They also attacked, at the same time, the United States Army Airfield at Hickam Field, which bordered the Pearl Harbor Navy Base.

Many sailors, and soldiers, lost their lives, and many were wounded. Many ships and airplanes were destroyed.

The next day, December 8, 1941, the United States declared war on the Empire of Japan.

I was a Junior in high school.

10

U. S. Marine Corps

One year, three months, and one day later, at the age of 17, after completing high school, I enlisted and was sworn into the United States Marine Corps.

I was in excellent physical condition. I had been an athlete in high school. I could swim more than a mile and I could run for hours without tiring.

While living in Annapolis, I was a member of the Navy Juniors, which was a forerunner of the Navy Junior R.O.T.C.

I had been trained by the Marines who were stationed at the United States Naval Academy.

I was an orphan, and contingent on my surviving the war in good health, I planned on making a career of being a Marine and retiring at the age of 47 with 30 years of service.

I was transported to the Marine Corps Recruit Depot at Parris Island, South Carolina, where I was to be taught how to become a U. S. Marine.

The training was, in a word, *rigorous.* It was both physically and mentally challenging at all times, day and night.

I relished it!
I was in my element!
Everything came easy for me!

When asked what type of duty I preferred after "boot camp" at Parris Island, I chose radio operator. Because radio was, at that time, the most advanced method of field combat communication.

After completion of my Basic Training at Parris Island, I was issued orders and transported to the Field Radio Operators School located at Camp Lejeune, North Carolina.

I had become a Marine!

We dressed for school as Marines!
We marched to school as Marines!

We walked like Marines!
We talked like Marines!
The course of study was demanding.
The instructors were demanding, but excellent.
We studied hard!
We worked hard!
We played hard!
We were polite.
We were courteous.
We looked good in our uniforms.
We felt good in our uniforms.

We were the Elite! And we knew it!
We were "the Few, the Proud."
We were—the Marines!

SEMPER FI
OOH RAH!
ONCE A MARINE!
ALWAYS A MARINE!

And through it all—
You, Lord Jesus were there with me.
You moderated my enthusiasm!
You reined in my foolish Pride!

And You reminded me that more trying and life-threatening trials may be in my future!

I thank You, Lord Jesus, for always being with me through "Thick or Thin." Your Friendship and Your Love are the Sustaining Force in my life!

I Thank You!!!

11

Letters

First Letter

As a student at Camp Lejeune, I had ample free time to write to Betty to renew our relationship.

In my first letter to her, I told her what had happened in my life since we were last together.

I told Betty that I was now thinking about her often each day, and that I was looking forward to seeing and spending some time with her again if she had similar desires.

I wrote that upon completion of my Radio Operators School training, I would be promoted to PFC and be given a leave from the Marine Corps so that I could visit relatives and friends before being sent to California for additional training and then be sent to the South and Central Pacific War Zones.

I wrote that I would very much enjoy spending a day or two with her while I was on leave as I had much I wanted to say to her before I was sent overseas.

I asked her if she would like me to come and visit with her and to please write and tell me what had happened in her life since last being together. Did she have a boyfriend?

First Reply

Three weeks later I received a nice letter from Betty that made me very happy. Thank You, Lord Jesus!!!

Betty wrote that because of the war, most sports activities with other schools had been stopped. Many sports and social activities at the school had been curtailed.

She would be a senior in high school starting in September.

She wrote that much of life had changed

because of the war. Everything was rationed, including most foods.

Travel was difficult because there were so many servicemen and women and they were given seating before civilians.

She only had one old pair of stockings remaining because they were not available. Nylon was being used to make parachutes.

There were no cars to buy and no gas to run old cars and no tires.

She asked if I had any pictures of myself that I could send her. She sent me two small pictures of herself with friends.

She did not write anything about me coming and visiting with her while I was on leave. She wrote nothing about boyfriends.

I read the letter slowly three times.

Second Letter (Box)

After reading her letter, I went to the PX (post exchange) on base and asked a male Marine clerk for some ladies nylon stockings. He said the PX did not have any but he could get me two pairs for fifteen dollars, cash in advance. I gave him fifteen dollars. He told me to return in two days.

Two days later he handed me a bag. I looked inside at two pairs of nylon stockings. I also bought a box of candy bars and a box of chewing gum.

The clerk gave me a box that was just the correct size for three items and packing material.

I placed three pictures of myself in the box also. Two pictures were of me in uniform and one of me in swimming trunks at the beach.

I mailed the box to Betty.

Second Reply

Ten days later, I received the letter that I was wanting and hoping to receive.

She thanked me for the stockings, candy, and gum. Then she thanked me for the stockings again.

I knew that the stockings would please her because at all times Betty tried to dress properly.

She wrote that she had given most of the candy and gum away to relatives and friends who had not had any lately. Aunt Hattie came to mind.

She was very pleased with the pictures that I

sent. I could almost hear her voice as she wrote, "You are no longer the boy that I knew. You have grown into a well-built man. You are so handsome in your uniform. I cannot wait to see you again. But, I will.

My eyes started to well with tears. This hardened Marine had been touched to his very soul.

I know, Lord Jesus, that it was Your doing this for your "angel" and me. I Thank You!!! I Thank You!! I Thank You!!!

Betty ended her letter with, "When will you get your leave and come to be with me?" Always, Betty.

I leaned back in my chair, sighed, and then laughed. I thought, "It was the uniform! The uniform always gets them!"

Third Letter

In my next letter to Betty, I wrote that I planned on arriving at her home at near noontime on Sunday, September 5, 1943.

Then I planned to leave Carvel Hall in Annapolis at 2:00 p.m. on Tuesday, September 7.

We would be together all day Labor Day, September 6.

I must report in at Camp Lejeune before 8:00 a.m. Wednesday, September 8, 1943.

I asked if I could sleep at her home while there.

I asked her to plan where and what she would like to do during my time with her.

I am anxious to see and be with you again.

I have much that I want to tell you before I go overseas.

Love, Paul

Third Reply

The last letter that I received from Betty while at Camp Lejeune was short and to the point. She wrote that there had been many changes in her family. She would tell me all when I came to be with her.

Because of so many war-time changes and restrictions, she just wanted she and I to be alone with each other and talk and get to know one another again as we had done when we were younger.

This was the Betty that I had remembered. Smart, thinking, and sensitive, with both feet on the ground and her head where it belonged.

I mailed her a box of chocolates with a happy birthday card wishing her a happy 17th birthday on August 22, 1943. I signed the card, "with much love, Paul."

12

Together Again

I arrived at Betty's home on Sunday, September 5, 1943.

Betty opened the door and there in front of me was "That Face!" She had become so beautiful that I was speechless for a few seconds.

We both knew in that instant that we were deeply in love with each other.

I held her closely to me and said softly, "Thank You, Lord Jesus!!!"

Then we kissed each other as two in love kiss! Unbelievable Joy!

I then spoke to her and said, "I am hopelessly and totally in love with you. And I have been since I first saw you at Annapolis High School two years ago."

She looked deep into my eyes with her beautiful hazel-colored eyes and said, "I am so happy and pleased that you are."

We walked arm in arm into the living room and sat close together on the sofa.

I sat my Marine Corps "ditty bag" on the floor beside me. I opened the bag and removed two pairs of nylon stockings.

I said as I presented her the stockings, "I thought that you could wear these at social functions at school this year."

She thanked me and kissed me again. Then she began touching my lips softly with her fingers as though she was examining them. She said, "Your kisses are magical. They relax me as though I haven't a care in the world. And they make me feel very good."

And then she started to well up with tears. I asked her why she was crying. I kissed her tears, then blotted her eyes and cheeks.

She said that a month or so previously she had read an article by a reporter that had been with the Marines at the Battle of Guadalcanal. In the article the reporter had said that all Japanese soldiers are taught to shoot and kill all Marines that carry radios on their backs because that was the main way Marine units communicated with each other.

Betty asked me if that statement was the truth.

I replied, "Yes, that is true, but we had contingency plans if that happened."

She said, "But you would be killed or wounded." She started to tear up again.

I knew I needed to say something that would calm her fears.

I replied, "There are many men around me to help keep that from happening. And I am trained to take protective measures for myself. Besides, I am very confident that I will be coming back and marrying you. I have this feeling because my Best Friend is always with me and He will protect me as He has done in the past, since I was five years of age. If you ask Him with all of your heart, He will answer your prayers. But you must trust in Him and not worry about something that you cannot control."

Love is the answer, because Love conquers all.

She had calmed down a little, smiled and said, "Of course you are speaking of Jesus."

I replied, "You know that I am."

She held both of my hands in hers, looked deep in to my eyes, and said, "Paul, I am totally yours and yours alone and I will be as long as I live."

I was stunned. I sat speechless. As I tried to get my mind around what she had just said, I felt like I was in another dimension.

Here we were, two seventeen-year-olds, speaking with and loving each other as though we were twenty-eight or thirty years old. We were seventeen in calendar years but thirty in our thought processes and emotions.

War has a way of aging people far beyond their chronological age.

I regained my composure. I gently pulled her up onto her feet. We embraced and kissed. I thanked her for her promise of love forever. Then I promised my love beyond death.

I took her by the hand and said, "Come with me."

We entered the kitchen, I said, "I know that

you all have restrictive food rationing, but this Marine needs something to eat!"

Betty replied, "I have planned for your visit and we have plenty of food. I have my contacts, you know."

I replied, "I'm sure that you do."

As we were preparing the food (soup and sandwiches) I said jokingly, "It sure did take us a long time to get to know each other again."

She replied, "Didn't it!" and we laughed.

Then we kissed. Then and there, at that moment, a pattern was set that lasted a lifetime.

Throughout our lifetime together, we would enjoy a good laugh at ourselves, and then hug and kiss.

And Oh!!! How I loved her!!! And Oh!!! How she loved me!!!

Betty was living alone at home most of the time. Her mother (Mabel) was employed as a twenty-four-hour a day nurse/companion for an elderly wealthy lady in Baltimore. She came home one day every ten days.

Aunt Hattie had remarried. She had married a man who was twenty years younger than herself.

Not long after their marriage, her husband was drafted into the Army and stationed in London, England.

Aunt Hattie was employed full-time as a receptionist/clerk at a mortuary that required her to live in an apartment that was part of the establishment so that she could answer the phone day and night.

Betty said Aunt Hattie would be with us about four hours on Labor Day, the next day, to cook and have dinner with us.

I was looking forward to being with Aunt Hattie again.

Betty suggested that I shave and shower early because no lights were allowed to be seen from outdoors at nighttime. It was hot and humid, there was no air conditioning. Only floor fans in each room. There were no street lights at night anymore, everything had to be darkened. All windows and doors had light-proof coverings at night and all indoor lighting had to be minimal light.

Only emergency vehicles were permitted on streets and highways at night, and they had special non-glare filtered headlights. The nation was at war and everyone had to stay alert in the event of an air raid or an attack.

It was early September. It was hot and humid with no air blowing outdoors. I had showered but I felt like I should fill the bathtub with cold water and sleep in it.

I asked Betty if they had a hot water bottle. She said yes and brought it to me. I emptied an ice tray of ice, crushed the ice small enough to fit into the water bottle. I wrapped a dishtowel around the bottle, took it into Betty, removed her slippers, then placed the bottom of her bare feet onto the bottle. She had observed my actions from the fan-filled living room while listening to "love" music on the radio.

Approximately ten minutes later, she said that her entire body was feeling cooler. I removed the rubber hot/cold water bottle from her feet, removed the towel, moved to the end of the sofa, placed the bottle on the floor with my feet on top. I asked her to turn on the sofa so that she could place her feet on to my lap, which she did. I began lightly massaging the bottoms of her feet. She said that it felt very, very good and felt as though it was relaxing her entire body. She said that she was very relaxed and did not feel overheated any longer.

Then she asked, "Where did you learn all this?"

I answered, "Don't you remember? I'm a 'country boy,' and we learned many more things from our home teachings than we learned in school."

We sat there and listened to and sang along with love songs they were playing on the radio. She fell asleep in my arms.

I carried her into her bedroom, placed her on the bed, and kissed her so as not to awaken her.

Then going to her mother's bedroom, I opened the air raid curtains and windows. A light, cooler breeze was blowing.

After returning to Betty's room and opening the curtains and windows there, I went to bed in her mother's room and we both slept soundly throughout the night.

I awoke at 5:30 the next morning, Labor Day. I showered and dressed halfway. I looked in at

Betty. She was fast asleep. I closed her bedroom door.

I opened all the curtains and windows in the house to let in the cool breeze.

Breakfast

I would prepare her breakfast of grapefruit, bacon and eggs, coffee, fried potatoes, and toast. I would serve breakfast in the breakfast nook part of the kitchen with a lighted candle in the center of the table.

I went and opened Betty's bedroom door.

She turned over, we said good morning, and she said, "What smells so good?"

I said, "You need to come to the kitchen for that answer. I suggest you brush your teeth, wash your face, and brush your hair because breakfast will be served in ten minutes."

She went to the bathroom and our conversation continued through the closed door.

"How many pieces of toast do you like?"

"One, and cut off the crust before you toast it."

"Are you hungry?"

"Yes, I didn't have any dinner last night."

"You did not cook any dinner last night."

"I don't know how to cook."

"Have Aunt Hattie teach you."

"She doesn't live here any longer."

"Can you read?"

"Yes."

"Then buy a cookbook."

She entered the kitchen and as usual I was amazed at her beauty.

I said, "There is a price to enter this kitchen."

"What is the price?"

"A hug and a kiss."

"Is that the appetizer?"

"Yes, and the same is the dessert."

"How do you like your eggs? I'm serving fried today. But I will serve you boiled or poached if you so desire."

"I will have them fried because you already have them in the skillet."

"I could eat four. I'm already the garbage can here with three pieces of toast plus crusts."

"I almost forgot to light the candle. Would you please ask the Lord to bless us and this food?"

"Oh, yes, yes. Bless us O Lord and this food

which we are receiving from Your bounty, through Jesus Christ Our Lord. Amen."

And I said, "Amen."

"Where did you learn to cook like this? Everything is cooked just the way I like it."

"How many times must I tell you?"

"Ok, ok, now I remember. You are a country boy."

Conversation after Breakfast

"Tell me, sweetheart, if you do not know how to cook, where and how do you eat?"

"I eat at Johnsons, across the street. I've eaten there since Fred died except when Aunt Hattie lived with us after Fred had died."

"Fred willed you that house in his will."

"Yes he did. Mr. Johnson was Fred's office manager at the Yacht Yard, and he drove Fred anyplace he needed to go, including back and forth to work. Fred permitted him and his family to live in the house rent free. After the Board had voted Mother out and then bought her out, Mother had permitted them to continue living in the house rent-free if they would permit me full access and feed me and take care of my needs. It has worked out well for me as they have two daughters who are friends of mine, one older and one younger than I."

"How do you get to the beauty parlor?"

"I have learned to take care of my hair myself. Mr. Johnson drives me to the beauty parlor once a month."

"Do you still have the charge plates at the department stores in Baltimore?"

"Yes, but I do not use them as much as I had previously."

"Do you keep any cash here at home?"

"Yes. We have a metal locked cash box that I have access to."

"Do you still have your friends here in your home for parties?"

"No, not since the war started."

"Do you date?"

"Yes, but not too often, about once every three weeks."

"Who do you date?"

"Only two nice boys from school, Henry Booker and Jack Ellis."

"Do they kiss you?"

"Yes. I only let them kiss me once goodnight. Henry is a good kisser. Jack wants to train for the Diplomatic Corps. Henry is going to join the Marines."

"Who else do you date?"

"I date men who are twenty years or older. One is twenty-six. And they all have their own cars."

"Do you kiss them?"

"Only once goodnight."

"Do you invite them into your house with you?"

"No, never."

"Do they make sexual advances?"

"Yes, but if they do, I never date them and have nothing to do with them again."

"You are one smart young lady."

"I am a virgin and I am saving myself for the man that I will marry."

"You know that if I survive the war and come home to you that I will marry you."

"Yes, and when you do return, I will marry you. I love you so very much."

"And I love you the same."

We stood, embraced, and kissed.

Aunt Hattie Again

"What time will Hattie be arriving?"

"Around noon."

"I will clean up the kitchen while you shower and get dressed."

"Ok. Do you want me to dry the dishes?"

"No, there's not enough time. I need to get dressed after you do."

Betty and I were all dressed.

Betty said, "Put your hat on as Aunt Hattie arrives. I want her to see you in your uniform."

I replied, "It is called a "cover," not a hat."

"Ok, but please put it on before she gets here."

A few minutes later, Hattie rang the doorbell. We opened the door and she entered. She and Betty hugged. Hattie turned to me, smiled broadly, and held my arms out at her arms' length.

She turned to Betty and said, "Look at him!

Who is he? Where did he come from? Are there anymore of them where he came from?"

Betty replied, "I knew you would be surprised."

Hattie said, "I am indeed and very pleased."

I said to both of them, "STOP IT!" then turned to Hattie and said, "Give me a hug."

She tried to squeeze the breath out of me.

She turned to Betty and said, "If he looks like this at seventeen, what will he look like at twenty?"

Betty said, "If you remain in this area, you will know because he will be living with me."

We entered the living room and Betty and I sat on the sofa, Hattie in a chair.

I said to Hattie, "Congratulations on your marriage. So tell me about your husband."

She replied, "He had worked at a hospital where I was previously employed, and there he kept after me to date him. So after about six months or so, he took me to dinner one evening. He was very nice and attentive. I would, on occasion later on, have dinner with him, until one evening, he told me that he loved me and had loved me for some time and wanted to be with me more often. His name was James Shenk. I left that job to come to be with Betty and Mabel after Fred died."

"After Mabel had lost the yacht yard business, I knew that I would be moving on. I answered an ad for a clerk/receptionist placed by a mortuary. I applied and was welcomed into the business. One of the other employees happened to be Jim Shenk. A big surprise to me. He would come to visit with me in my apartment which was part of the mortuary. His name was on the military draft list for the armed forces. He wanted to marry before going into the Army."

"I finally relented and said yes, even though he was twenty years younger than me. He was a very nice and considerate man. I thought that he would be a good husband for me."

I said to her, "Was his mother living?"

Betty yelled, "PAUL!"

Hattie smiled, then we both began laughing.

I looked at Betty and said, "Laugh, sweetheart!"

She then joined in the laughter.

I then asked Hattie, "Is she older than you?"

Laughingly, Hattie answered, "Not by much. Maybe a year or two."

We all had another good laugh.

Betty laughingly said to me, "You're tooooo much!"

I replied, "I needed to know."

I put on my serious face, then said to Hattie, "I know that you know all the particulars so please tell me why and how Mabel lost the yacht yard business."

She replied, "It was awful. Fred died and willed the business to Mabel and Betty. All of his majority stock went to Mabel so she became president of the company. Mabel knew little to nothing about running a business or finances. I even had to balance her personal checkbook for her for years prior to her marrying Fred."

"After the will was probated and read, Mabel foolishly felt her importance. She was the head of a company and she would run it her way. I cautioned her and tried to advise her. She told me it was none of my business. But I advised her to get a good lawyer in Baltimore. She told me the company lawyer was a very good, nice man from Washington D.C who was presently wining and dining her. I told her that she was being set up for a fall, so be very careful. I told her to be wary of her office manager Mr. Johnson, who lived in Betty's house across the street, who also drove her to the yard several times each week. I knew about her arrangement with the Johnson's concerning Betty eating and having access to her house. Mabel's relatives and past friends started coming out of the woodwork, repeatedly asking to borrow money and never repaying any of it. She was an "easy mark" for anyone who had a sad story, be it true or false."

"Valuable, highly skilled craftsmen were leaving the yard. It was all planned, of course. Business fell off badly. Large, loyal accounts were taking their business elsewhere. Twice her nice dinner companion/Washington lawyer convinced her to sell him large portions of her company stock. She had been had!"

"Her lawyer friend had become majority stockholder and president of the company. She was voted off the Board of Directors, offered a buyout at a ridiculously low price. She felt she had no choice. She accepted and was completely out of the business."

"The yacht yard now has a very lucrative contract building PT boats for the United States Navy."

"Mabel presently has a twenty-four hour a day nurse/companion job nursing a wealthy lady and Betty has lost her security of a lifetime."

Betty said, "That is the first time I have heard the complete story."

I said to Betty, "Do not concern yourself about it. I will take care of you for as long as you live."

Aunt Hattie cooked a delicious dinner which we all enjoyed. She would need to leave by 4:30 PM to be home before dark. There was a war on.

Hattie hugged me and kissed me on the cheek again and said that she would pray for me daily.

I thanked her for the meal and her love and asked her to check on my sweetheart Betty as often as possible. She said she would and departed.

Betty and I were alone. I said to Betty, "I feel as though all of the wind has been taken out of my sails."

She replied, "I feel exactly the same way."

We turned the radio to Love Songs, laid on the sofa together in each other's arms. I told her that I wanted her to keep dating as needed but to be careful.

Even though we believe this war is a just war, war itself is evil. War will deceive and tempt you and if you are not on guard, it will steal away your moral resolve. But if you stay close, very close, to Jesus, He will protect you at all times.

She said, "I will."

Time to Say Goodbye

We fell asleep on the sofa in each other's arms. We awoke at 11:30 and went to bed separately.

I awoke at 5:30 am, shaved and showered, dressed, packed my bags, and then looked in on Betty. She was awake. I kissed both her cheeks and her forehead. She arose and showered then dressed into a beautiful Kelly green suit. With her hazel eyes she was so beautiful.

We ate cereal and toast and juice for breakfast.

We sat on the sofa facing each other. We had said all that needed saying. We kept looking into each other's eyes as though we were seeing each other's souls. Now and then, we would kiss. We were imprinting each other's face into our brain and into our souls.

We took the train to Annapolis. We sat together holding hands in Carvel Hall just looking into each other's eyes, now and then saying to each other, "I love you."

The bus arrived at 1:45 pm. I wanted to be the last to get on. We walked to the bus hand in hand. We embraced and kissed with an embrace and a kiss to last until we knew not when.

I whispered, "I love you" in her ear.

She whispered in mine, "And I love you."

I boarded the bus.

As it pulled away, she was there alone, waving goodbye.

And Oh! How I Loved Her!!!
And Oh! How She Loved Me!!!
And Oh! How We Loved Each Other!!!

13

Leaving the Corps

It was early August. I had been a patient on a troop carrier/hospital ship from Guam to Hawaii.

I was hospitalized in Hawaii five days, then placed in the infirmary of an aircraft carrier that was leaving Pearl Harbor for the United States.

I arrived at a Navy Base near Oakland, California. They took me off the carrier to a Naval Hospital near Pleasanton, California.

I was treated at that hospital for my severe headaches and the doctors said, "Combat Fatigue." They said I had been "shell-shocked."

After a few months, I was nauseated much of the time and losing weight. My headaches were becoming less frequent but lost none of their intensity.

After months with minimal improvement in my health, I was summoned to my doctor's office where I was told that my case was being reviewed by a group of doctors.

My doctor, a very nice man, came and took me into a boardroom where five other doctors were seated at a long table. I was ushered to a seat. My doctor sat facing me. He then told me that he and the board of doctors had reviewed my records and had discussed my case. He then said the board had determined that my condition had not improved to the point where I could go back to active duty and that I would be discharged from the Marine Corps because of a medical disability. He said that the Veterans Administration would provide my medical care in the future without cost to me.

I would be transferred to a Navy Convalescent Hospital which in reality was a resort hotel leased by the Navy. I had my choice of three hotels. Sun Valley, Idaho. The Broadmoor in Colorado Springs, Colorado. Or the Casa del Rey in Santa

Cruz, California. I chose the Casa del Rey because of the many employment opportunities in California at that time.

On December 4, 1944, I was transferred to Santa Cruz. The weather in Santa Cruz at that time of year did not agree with me.

On Wednesday, the 20th of December, I was diagnosed with pneumonia and pleurisy and placed in "sick bay" at the hotel. I was discharged from sick bay on December 28.

On Friday, February 2, 1945, I was transferred to the Marine Corps Detachment at the Moffett Field Naval Air Station located in Mountain View, California.

I was processed out of the Marine Corps on February 9, 1945. My career as a Marine ended twenty-eight years earlier than planned.

I was sick and heading to a home that was non-existent. A home was in my plans for the immediate future.

14

Coming "Home" to Betty

On my journey to be with my Betty, I stopped in Pittsburgh, Pennsylvania, to visit with two of my sisters and to check out the University of Pittsburgh.

I purchased some civilian clothing in Pittsburgh.

Betty and I had spoken on the phone once a month while I was in California. I called her from Pittsburgh and told her that I planned on arriving at her home the early afternoon of Monday, the 26th of February.

Most of my thoughts were of being with her again. I still did not feel too well and I had lost about forty pounds and I had a few gray hairs at my temples. I was nineteen years of age.

It had been one and a half years since we were last together.

It was cold weather and I was wearing my Marine green uniform which is worn in colder weather. It is a sharp-looking uniform, but not as visually attractive as summer khakis or the formal Marine "Blues" uniform.

I rang the doorbell. The door seemed to open immediately and there again was "That Face" with a huge smile.

She was no longer that beautiful seventeen year old that I had said goodbye to a year and a half earlier.

She was now a mature-looking, very beautiful, "sophisticated lady."

Before I could close the door, she leaped into my arms. We embraced and kept kissing each other.

I kept saying softly over and over again, "Thank You, Sweet Jesus, Thank You, Sweet Jesus," as streams of tears ran down our faces.

I was drying her tears ... She stepped back ... ... I closed the door.

She kept feeling my face lightly with her hand. She felt my arms, my chest, my back.

She said, "Your face is so thin, you have a touch of gray hair at your temples, your chest is thinner, your back is thinner."

Her voice kept getting louder and louder.

Then she yelled loudly, "WHAT HAS THIS TERRIBLE WAR DONE TO MY DARLING PAUL?"

Tears were streaming down my face.

I said to her, "Do I look that badly? Maybe I should not have come back."

She looked stunned.

She slumped to the floor on her knees weeping uncontrollably.

She wrapped both her arms around my legs and clutched them with all of her strength.

She said, "Oh, Paul, my darling Paul, what have I just done to you? I am so sorry, so very sorry for what I said. You are not well and I have inflicted more pain on you because of my selfishness. Please, please forgive me."

"Lord Jesus, I am so thankful to You for

bringing my darling Paul back to me and look what I have done to him. How can I make amends for my selfishness? Forgive me, Lord. Lord, please forgive me."

I had heard enough!

I gently pulled her to her feet, kissed her, picked her up in my arms, and carried her to the sofa in the living room.

I said to her, "I hope your mother and new stepfather are not in this house and hearing all of this."

She replied, "They would think that we are two crazy people."

I replied, "We are. We are crazy in love with each other. By the way, when will your Mother and stepfather be arriving back home?"

"Saturday."

"I will leave on Wednesday and return on Sunday to be with you."

"Ok."

"I am living with Uncle Lloyd in Washington until I find an apartment here in Baltimore."

"Mother bought an apartment house with some of her buyout money. She has a vacancy."

I said, "That may be a temporary housing solution. You work at the Baltimore Sun newspaper?"

"Yes, in Classified Advertising, Monday through Friday."

I answered, "When I am free, I will take you to lunch or dinner."

"You really know how to please a girl."

"My pleasure, Ma'am, but there will be the usual charge."

"A hug and a kiss?"

"You are a quick learner!"

We kissed.

She said, "I felt that kiss down to my toes. You may have lost forty pounds but none of your touch."

I replied, "We have an old country saying …"

She interrupted, "You are always full of old country sayings. What is it?"

I replied, "It takes a lean horse to run a great race."

She replied, "I like that, so I will stay thin and you are already thin."

I said, "It should be a great race."

"It will be," she said.

I asked, "Is our love back to where it should be?"

She replied, "Oh, yes. Oh, yes."

We kissed again.

I said, "It sure did take a long time, didn't it?"

She said, "Didn't it?"

We were both back to where we belonged, and we knew it.

"By the way, did you buy a cookbook?"

"No, I did not."

"Did you learn how to cook?"

"Not yet. I eat dinner here now that Mother cooks for Bill."

"Can you boil water?"

"Maybe."

"We will start the cooking school in one hour."

"Ok."

We sealed all with an embrace and a kiss that will never end.

I removed my Marine Corps uniform for the last time that evening.

We would love and plan our future life together, looking forward to whatever was in store for us.

15

My HERO

Failing Health

Two years after being told by my doctor and the Patient Review Board at the Pleasanton, California Naval Hospital that I would be discharged by the hospital and the Marine Corps because of my service-incurred medical disability, my health was declining rapidly.

I was in school and training under the G. I. Bill. In late August of 1946, I went to the Baltimore V.A. Office and told them that I felt very ill.

The V.A. doctors gave me their complete physical examination, including laboratory and x-ray examinations. They told me it was all due to my "Combat Fatigue." I did not agree with their diagnosis, and I told them so.

In the first week of October, 1946, every time I coughed, blood came up and out of my mouth.

I needed to do something quick.

I slowly boiled in water an empty jam jar and lid. I cooled them. As the fluids with blood were coughed up, I spit them into the jar and sealed the jar with the lid.

One day later, I called on a friend who worked as a lab tech for the Maryland State Laboratory. I needed a favor. I asked her to culture the contents of the jar, then call and report the results to our family physician. She said that she would.

On my 21st birthday, our family physician called me with devastating news.

I had four plus active pulmonary tuberculosis.

My family physician said he would notify the V.A. and said the V.A. would send an ambulance for me.

In my opinion, the Navy and V.A. doctors' diagnosis was incomplete.

I placed myself in isolation with Betty the only

one to have access to my room. The ambulance arrived one week later.

After admittance to a V.A. hospital and tests, the final diagnosis was: far advanced bilateral pulmonary tuberculosis involving two lobes in each lung with cavitation in the left upper lobe.

Betty and I had been blessed with a beautiful baby boy who was a few months old.

Betty had a day to vent her shock and tears. Her resolve came to the fore.

She said with resolute determination, "You will get well! I will not let this defeat us."

"I will pray and pray and devote all of my energy caring for you, and will also see that you are taken care of properly."

"You WILL beat this disease!"

"I will *WILL* you well! This disease will not take you from me!"

Betty's love and actions and devotion over the next eight years proved to me that she really was what I always had known her to be.

She really was an angel that You, Lord Jesus, had sent to this earth to be one with me forever.

All of my Heroes in my life were the dead

Marines and other dead military men and women and civilians who had given up their lives for family and friends here at home. I had no living heroes who had not made the ultimate sacrifice. Military or civilian persons of all eras who had grand monuments to honor them but who had not given their lives were not "heroes" to me.

I now had to make an exception to this and modify my opinion.

I had a new Hero who, if possible, I would crown with the "Wreath of Victory" and a civilian Medal of Honor for Love, Devotion, and Service Above and Beyond her Vow of Love Completely, Forever.

MY BEAUTIFUL WIFE BETTY.

Who is beyond "PRECIOUS" TO ME.

From that day forward, throughout our lifetime together, I, and I alone, called her

PRECIOUS

And Oh! How I Love Her!!!
And Oh! How I Will Always Love Her!!!

We Thank You, Lord Jesus!!!
We Will Constantly
Thank You, Lord Jesus!!!

16

Type A and Type B Personalities

Precious possessed a Type B personality. Mine was a classic Type A. We were aware of these differences prior to our marriage. We determined that if they opposed each other from time to time, we believed that our Love would be strong enough to override and resolve differing opinions. As an example, my returning from service in the Marine Corps during WWII during which ten months were served in combat zones followed by six months in Naval hospitals as a patient, I possessed a very "short fuse" and a "quick temper" that had the potential of becoming violent. I would never direct this behavior at Precious. Never! On two occasions prior to our marriage, this character weakness exhibited itself. One was only a short, temporary "short fuse," followed by a stern warning. The other was violent that resolved itself in less than five seconds. Both incidents happened with former suitors of Precious who foolishly challenged my notice that Precious was mine and would become my wife.

I knew this problem of mine and I worked to control it. Precious was of great assistance in my effort to do so. I knew some of the reasons it was such.

During our first twenty-four years of marriage, Precious, being her sweet, loving, type B, developed a simple but effective way of defusing my anger whenever it reared its ugly head. She would simply say, "All right, Fury, don't you think that is enough?" It always worked. My fury would abate. Lovingly, she would then hug and kiss me and say, "My old Fury." She was amazing. And Oh! How I Loved her for it!!!

As You know, Sweet Jesus, after the sale of the farm, when I asked You to change me and You answered my plea and You did change me, the so-called "short fuse" and "quick temper" were gone.

I Thank You, Lord Jesus. I Thank You!!! Your changing me was the blessing Precious and I needed to blend two opposing personalities into one. We termed it an AO personality. Our Thanks is Eternal!!!

17

Art, Music, Literature, Writing, Reading, Nature

Art was in the genes of Precious. Many of her paternal ancestors had been artists of various renown. Precious had the ability to write or draw or paint with either hand. As others in her grandparents' household produced works of art, Precious would observe them and practice her own drawing or painting.

In high school, she was a member of the art club and was the artist for the school's monthly newsletter. She dabbled in art throughout her lifetime until the infirmities of age prevented her from doing so.

During our lifetime together, Precious and I chose to travel extensively in part of the United

States and a small part of Mexico. Precious was a prolific writer of letters to relatives and friends. On the back of each sealed envelope, Precious would sketch a scene of whatever area we were visiting at that time.

Whenever Precious saw something that "caught her eye," she would draw it or sketch it. Be it animal, vegetable, or mineral, nothing was too grand or too mundane to draw.

Precious and I were bound together as one by many aspects of life. We thoroughly treasured and enjoyed all. As You know, Lord Jesus, our love and faith and trust in You was and is paramount in our lives. Followed by our love for each other and our family. These and all other aspects of life blended into one beautiful milieu of The Song and Dance of Life!

Music played an important role in our Dance of Love. There was music playing as we were first together in that gazebo when Precious was fourteen years of age. In that gazebo I had asked her what type of music she liked. She had answered, "All types." So "all types" were in our entire life.

Giacomo Puccini was the favorite operatic composer of Precious. Also mine. La Bohème was her favorite opera, followed closely by Madame Butterfly. The same applied for me.

Her favorite classical composition was Intermezzo from Cavalleria Rusticana composed by Pietro Mascagni. Mine was Meditation from Thaïs composed by Jules Massenet.

Our favorite aria, sung by a soprano, was O Mio Babbino Caro from Gianni Schicchi composed by Puccini and sung by Montserrat Caballé.

Our favorite aria, sung by a tenor, was Nessun Dorma from Turandot composed by Puccini as sung by our favorite tenor of all time Luciano Pavarotti.

Our favorite symphony: Symphony No. 9 by Ludwig van Beethoven. Our favorite stage musical: The Sound of Music, written by Richard Rogers and Oscar Hammerstein II.

We also enjoyed many "ditties" from around the world. Precious always had music nearby. In the kitchen, living room, bedroom. We had a radio in the barn, automobiles, trucks, boat, and all RVs.

Our very favorite type of music was, you guessed it: Love Songs! Every day that we were together we would recite, hum, sing, or whistle Love Songs. Love Songs were like another language to us that only she and I, and You Lord Jesus, could understand. As an example, occasionally we would speak only using song titles. We would be sitting quietly, then all of a sudden I would say to her "I Think of You." Then I would connect my cell phone to my large speakers, tap Perry Como singing "I Think of You" as only Perry could sing it. Followed by "And I Love You So" with Perry singing.

Then quickly, because of tears, I would play Andrea Bocelli's album entitled "Passione," which would elicit our desire to embrace, kiss, and dance! It was a "game" that we had played throughout most of our life with different singers and/or music. The effects and feelings produced by these musical Games of Love were always, as they say, "Magical!"

Almost every night, Precious and I would,

during our "pillow talk" and afterwards, go to sleep with "Love Music" playing softly.

Three weeks before her death, I was in the kitchen preparing a light meal for Precious, who at that time was only eating one spoonful of anything. Precious was sitting in her chair in our sitting room. As I was cooking I was softly whistling "Mimi's Aria" from "La Bohème." I heard the sound of shuffling slippers, turned around, and there was my Precious, in her weakened condition, coming toward me. I rushed to aid her. She said to me, "I heard what you were whistling and I had to come and have you hold me." I held her, as I always held her while standing, with her head in the same spot on my chest where she had always placed it. It was an embrace of a lifetime of Love. We kissed with tears flowing, and Oh! How we loved each other!!! I Thank You, Lord Jesus! I Thank You!!!

I assisted her back to her chair. She was very weak. I served her lunch, she ate one bite. I kissed her on her lips and on her forehead. She went off to sleep.

I sat and watched her. Was Precious in her

manner, imitating You, Lord Jesus? As a teenager, she had read a little book which I had reread to her. A little book that had been written centuries before by a monk by the name of Thomas á Kempis entitled "The Imitation of Christ." Was my Precious, during her three years of suffering, imitating Your suffering?

Faith and Nature

After Faith, Love, and Family came Learning. Learning from all aspects of life and living. Faith and Nature are schools where one can attend class and learn throughout your lifetime.

Each school has its own set of rules and regulations that are necessary for the common good of all. There is only one animal that causes discord in these two schools. That animal is homo sapiens. Men and women from all areas of the earth.

Precious and I tried to attend class each and every day at both schools.

Because of our attendance record, we have been rewarded beyond our wildest hopes and dreams. For example, of rewards received: we have been privileged to witness a sunrise that encompassed the entire sky from east to west.

Also to view a sunset that encompassed the entire sky from west to east.

To view the Milky Way and the Cosmos from a mountain top over 10,000 feet high with no obstruction caused by man-made lighting or air pollutants.

The sky, daytime or nighttime, was always a source of great beauty to Precious. The sky appeared in most of her drawings.

The rewards of constant attendance in the Schools of Faith and Nature are endless.

Peace of mind, in any and all situations.
Discernment, negation of desires and fears.
Peace of soul.
Love of all, equally and unconditionally.

"Ask and it will be given to you.
Seek and you will find.
Knock and the door will be opened to you."
Matthew 7:7

Continue asking!
Continue seeking!
Continue knocking!

The intentions of your heart and your type of
prayer are your key to opening the door to

GOD *IS* LOVE
1 John 4:8-16

A Prolific Reader

Precious was a prolific reader. At one time,
she possessed library cards from five different
libraries in five cities or towns.

In 1999, she lost much of her eyesight due to
the wet type of age-related macular degeneration.
The latest treatment modalities were never
able to permanently curtail the bleeding. The
scarring from the use of hot and cold lasers was a
detriment to later advanced treatments. Plus her
allergic reaction to some medications used and her
anxiety ruled out pursuing further treatments. As
always, she made the final decision. This "angel"
who had nursed and comforted so many was now
inconsolable. She cried sometime every day for

one year. My heart ached for her. Her eyesight meant much of life to her.

It was a journey. She could no longer drive a car, she couldn't cook as she had done. The places and people she could no longer see and she could no longer read! No more mending, sewing, no calligraphy, no more map reading as copilot/navigator.

Large print books, books on tape, large TVs, we tried those and all else until final acceptance. Never full, one hundred percent acceptance. Ninety percent is more realistic. No more reading poetry! Oh my! Poe, Service, Longfellow, Etc. No more reading the Book of all books, the Bible. Douay-Rheims, the King James, the NIV, the Revised New American, and the Jerusalem. After the failure of her eyesight, I read to her daily from the Bible and many other books, mostly concerning Faith in God.

Because of the Great Depression of the late 1920s and 1930s, Precious and I were introduced separately to a rural style of living. She about twenty miles from Baltimore, and I in the far western county of Maryland. Her grandparents, with whom she lived, moved from the city of Baltimore to a small farm located five miles beyond the town of Laurel, Maryland. I spent summers with my mother's parents who owned a farm near Friendsville, in Garrett County in far western Maryland.

Both farms were near creeks and rivers. Placing each of us in such an environment was like "putting ducks into water." We each thoroughly embraced and enjoyed it. The flora and fauna of each region was soaked up like a sponge in both of us.

Precious as a nine year old rescued three skunk kits whose mother had been killed by a motor vehicle, a female and two males. She raised them to adulthood. The female chose the male she would mate with. Then she and her chosen mate killed the other male by stripping him of his hide. A lesson in Nature well-learned. She learned why guinea hens make such good watch dogs. The same as a peacock.

We learned that all those foodstuffs in food stores did not originate wrapped in plastic or paper. Likewise with much of the medicine in drugstores. My dear grandmother taught me how to identify and harvest medicinal herbs to ship to pharmaceutical companies to be used in medicines. Foxglove, witch hazel, mayapple, and ginseng, to name a few. There are in the United States many varieties of wild mushrooms, but fewer than half of them are edible. We learned that flora and fauna varied with each life zone as defined by altitude. Nature had its rules, but men and women were going to attempt to change them, come what may.

Precious and I were drawn to Nature. All of it. Consequently, when our son Michael was sixteen and our daughter Maureen was nine years of age, Precious and I decided that we should leave a comfortable home in suburban Baltimore and look to live on a farm. We would take our time and get what we wanted. The first requirement would be water. The second, tillable land, then pasture and timber. There must be a wooded area of good size.

We perused the farms for sale in the classified section in the Washington Post and Baltimore Sun for several months. We ruled out most of Maryland and Delaware. We ruled out the Atlantic coastal plain and Appalachia. We decided on the Piedmont region of Virginia. Then once again, Lord Jesus, You provided what we were both looking for.

18

A Real Natural Woman

At the time of our marriage, Precious was five feet three and one half inches tall and weighed ninety-eight pounds. She was nineteen years of age and she was beautiful!

And Oh! How I Loved her!

Fifteen years later, after giving birth to two children and at the age of thirty-four years, my Precious came into "full bloom" physically and she remained in full bloom until she reached the age of forty-eight. She was stunningly attractive in all aspects of her being. A complete woman both inwardly and in her outward appearance. The wonderful part of it all was that she always considered herself only an average-looking person.

What a wonderful world this would be if there were more like her!

And Oh! How I Loved her!

Her concern and compassion for all others was exemplary and a marvel to behold. Our Lord Jesus bestowed on Precious the much desired and rare gift of "Common Sense." Her exercise of Common Sense was amazing and it was her forte.

However, if Precious witnessed someone unjustly insulting or abusing another person, the incident would "ignite the fire" that simmered within her and she was quick to defend the one receiving the ill treatment.

In the end, she would usually be the peacemaker for all. My Precious was a genuine natural woman who loved everyone and everyone loved her.

19

Laughter

Precious and I were you might say, rather reserved, relaxed, serious-minded wife and husband. Together we possessed one surprising quirk. We laughed a lot, every day.

We would find humor in situations that were not normally humorous. Our children and grandchildren learned to laugh a lot with us.

We are not sure that "laughter" is the best medicine in this time of scientific advancement. We were sure of one quality of laughter. Laughter in all probability is the best natural stress reducer that is available to all at no cost. And most of us should know, or be aware of, the harmful effects that prolonged or excessive stress has upon the human body and mind.

20

The Farm

One hundred acres on rolling land with a river at the back of the property. There were sixteen springs, one of which was an artesian sand spring. All formed three streams flowing into the river. Twenty acres of pasture, twenty acres of cleared tillable land, with the remainder in second and third growth timber, plus an old rundown cemetery plot.

The house was old but very substantial. It had eight rooms which were all the same size, sixteen foot by sixteen foot by eight foot high ceilings. There was or had been a fireplace in each room. There were two chimneys with four flues in each chimney. There was a well that was ninety-two feet to water, and then twenty-six feet of water. The well would never run dry under any conditions. Oh yes. The house had a seven-foot-wide center hallway both upstairs and downstairs. The entire property needed extensive repair.

Precious and I would soon find out what we were made of. We stocked the farm with Angus cattle, one milk cow, hogs, a small flock of sheep (for Precious), chickens (she loved her chickens), ducks, two horses, dogs, cats, and much native wildlife that used the property as their home.

Precious required that all domestic animals have a name. All of her sheep had French names except the first lamb was named Sunday because she was born on a Sunday. The ram was named Pierre. She named the one set of kittens Peaches, Clyde, Bonnie, C. W. Moss, and Tobias. She bought me a puppy for my birthday. I named him Caesar Augustus. We called him Augie. The Holstein milk cow's name was Vickie, the Angus bull was McDuff. The horses, Jocks Ann and Twiggy.

How precious was my Precious. And Oh! How I Loved her!

Precious had two playgrounds: her half-acre

vegetable garden and her sixty foot by ten foot flower bed. Our home became the pride and joy of Precious. Especially the dining room, the kitchen, and the living room. We remodeled the home and refurbished the land. We were pleased and knew that when we would leave the property, it would be in much better condition than when we purchased it.

Precious and I were always aware of the balance that prevails in all of life. We knew that with all the love of our chosen lifestyle on a farm, we would need to work long hours. That would require much blood, sweat, and tears. I had learned as a child of five years of age that "everything has a price." And we all must pay that price, eventually.

While living at the farm, I was employed as a manufacturer's representative, representing twelve companies. I was also employed by the University of Virginia as the Technical Director of the School of Radiologic Technology. I also owned a small General Contracting business. I enjoyed work and was a "workaholic."

After five consecutive years of a continuing severe drought and a disastrous drop in the price of prime beef at the stockyards, I was convinced that we should stop farming. Precious vehemently disagreed with my decision.

Our son Michael had enlisted in the Marine Corps and was in Viet Nam with his tour of duty to end soon after his return to the USA. He came home on leave and stated that he was not interested in the farmhouse or property.

At the same time, the final violent battle for my soul between the forces of Heaven and Hell that began at five years of age when my father came home with our cruel stepmother, was raging. Precious knew and was aware of this battle that raged within me. Our love was about to face its ultimate test.

I started liquidating the farm. Each time a group of animals sold, Precious lost more of her animal friends and it was all my fault. The process was heart wrenching for her. Watching the effect on Precious was heart wrenching for me. With each sale, I could see her disappointment in my actions increasing. OUR LOVE WAS UNDER SEIGE. It became unbearable. I moved out.

Foolishly, I began spending time with a

younger nurse friend of Precious who Precious had entertained at our home on several occasions. Her friend had broken the ninth commandment of God. A trait in some people that Precious found deplorable. Precious thought my actions were inexcusable. She was angry and voiced her disgust with me. I had no defense. I was flat out GUILTY!

Mike had been discharged from the Marine Corps. Rather than reenlist, he chose to come home. To a home that was falling apart. Mike did not want the house or the property.

I placed the farm up for sale. Precious rented a home in town for herself, Mike, and Maggie, and her pet Pekingese, which I had given her.

The farm sold before long. I financed the note for the new owner with Precious as co-note holder. We divided the profits equally.

I ended my association with the nurse/ex-friend.

Precious and I said "goodbye" and we went our separate ways. We both had deep wounds which needed to be healed. Precious was forty-two years of age. I was forty-three. And Oh! How I Loved her!!! And Oh! How she Loved me!!!

21

The Separation

I purchased a new RV and relocated to eastern North Carolina about an hour's drive to the Atlantic Ocean. It was springtime and I needed to prepare myself for a new life.

But first I needed to do a thorough spring-cleaning of myself. With much soul searching and much help from You, Lord Jesus, I realized that I had become the type of man that I did not care to be around. I was guilty of all of the things that I had found lacking in others. I really did not like myself. I had become disgusting to myself. I could now join my profound lament with that of St. Paul as he candidly describes his lament in Romans 7:15-25.

I needed changing! I felt that the efforts of

no man or woman were capable of changing me. After many hours and days and nights of repentance, mea culpas, and copious tears, with total Trust in You, Lord Jesus, I asked You to change me. Please, Lord Jesus, mold me into the type of man that will be acceptable to You. My prayers for Precious and our children were constant.

After two months in North Carolina alone, I called Precious and told her I wanted to come and talk with her.

She was as happy but reserved, to see me, as I was to see her. The children acted as though I had never been gone.

Praise be to Jesus!!! My thanks is Eternal! And Oh! How I Loved her!!!

22

How Do You Mend
a Broken Heart?

Later that evening, on my knees with tears flowing, I promised my Precious that I would not knowingly do anything to cause her heart to ache for the remainder of her life. I sealed my promise by removing her shoes and stockings and I kissed each one of her feet three times.

That was fifty years ago. Since that moment, many who know us, know that each day, I kneel before my Precious, remove her shoes/slippers and socks, and I kiss each foot three times. I will continue to kiss her feet each day as a reminder of my promise. And Oh! Lord Jesus, how I Love her!!!.

23

The Magnetism of Love

P recious and I were opposites, especially during the first twenty-four years of marriage. As all know, opposites attract, likes repel. We were like two magnets. Whenever two magnets are misaligned, they repel each other. When aligned properly, they bond together as one more powerful magnet.

In our earlier years we bonded as one ninety percent of the time. After twenty-four years of marriage, we came to the realization that we both desired and needed to be permanently bonded one hundred percent of the time. Most scholars regarded this ideal as an impossibility and nothing more than "wishful thinking." Precious and I were going to attempt to prove them and the other "naysayers" wrong. We were confident and we were trusting.

My ultimate quest since my childhood was a deep personal relationship with my Best Friend and my God, Jesus, whom I believed to be the Christ. I not only wanted to know all about Him, I wanted a close, a very close, personal relationship.

Because of several different than norm, "spiritual experiences" that occurred in my life, (Precious had witnessed a few), I was judged by some as weird, bizarre, double minded and other classifications, even though I walked and talked and acted and reacted and still put my pants on one leg at a time like all others. I had held positions of trust, leadership, my job performance always had high ratings. I was considered by most a nice guy who was on the serious side.

I was always polite and courteous to all, but I expected everyone to perform their duties to the best of their ability. All were graded or rewarded commensurate with their performance. The words "can't" and "mediocrity" were not in my vocabulary. Effort and proficiency were recognized and rewarded. I never required anyone to do anything I would or could not do myself.

Precious was the opposite. She strived for excellence but if it was not achieved it was acceptable with her. She accepted everyone on "face value." If one was too lazy or recalcitrant, Precious would do their duties for them, with limitations, of course. Precious was likely to permit an unpleasant situation to resolve itself with time. I was analytical, took action, and resolved it ASAP.

I cooked with measurement, time and temperature. Precious cooked by pinch, spoonful in hand, "throw it all together" and "touch." She was fantastic. Her cooking always had better flavor than mine. I used her method whenever I made soups. She told people that my soups had a better flavor than her soups. It was not true, of course. She said it to make me feel good so that I would do more cooking.

The one area where Precious and I became a perfect meld or blend starting in our twenty-fifth year of marriage was in our Love. Once I asked Precious to describe in one word her description of my love for her. She thought for about one minute, then said, "Intense." Then she asked me the same question. I replied, "Still or Quiet." From an old adage I had learned from my grandmother: "Still waters run deep." The Love of Precious ran deep to the very core of her being. And Oh! How I Loved her!!!

Our Love had survived an horrific storm. By the Love and Grace of my God, I had been "transformed by the renewal of my mind" as St. Paul urges all of us in Romans 12:2. I now knew the Source of the "Still" Love of Precious and the "Intense" Love of mine. I told Precious I would start a new "Five-Year Plan" that would end on my forty-eighth birthday. She looked at me, thought for a minute or so, smiled as only she could smile at me, then said, "I am in! Go for it!" My Precious was back! Thank You, Lord Jesus!!! And Oh!!! How I Loved her!!!

Mike chose to remain in Virginia to be near his future wife. Maggie would be entering her junior year of high school. We needed to relocate before the school year began. I had terminated all my work and business affairs at the time I sold the farm.

We relocated to a town of 36,000 population in Eastern North Carolina. I had taken a position as Chief Technologist in the Radiology Department of a new hospital. After two and a half months on the job I knew that the position was not a good fit for me. We stayed until the end of the school year. Then we relocated to the Baltimore area where Maggie could complete her last year of schooling. I renewed my Maryland General Contractor's license.

One weekend Precious and I decided on a drive across the Chesapeake Bay to sightsee in an area that we had not visited since we were newlyweds. Much of the produce sold in Baltimore comes from farms located on the Eastern Shore of Maryland. We drove to a small town located on the shore of the Chester River. We stopped at a quaint general store and entered. We were greeted warmly and were pleasantly surprised by the large variety of fresh and quality foods on sale in this little store. The cheese selection attracted my attention. Ages of cheeses ranged from six months, nine months, twelve months, to eighteen months. We chose a sample of the one-year old black rind. I knew at first taste that I surely would be back to this place of business.

We drove into Chestertown, thirty miles down the river, and noticed a hospital. I decided to stop and check out the facility. We entered though the ER entrance knowing that the Radiology Department would be nearby. The Chief Tech was on duty. I introduced Precious and myself and I liked the manner of this man. He asked my background. I said that I had been nationally registered for many years. He stated that no techs in the department were registered, not even himself. He offered me a job if I could start within a week or two. He called the radiologist for me to speak with. The radiologist said that he would prefer that Paul remain in charge. I said "No problem. As long as they paid the salary that I requested." Monday afternoon, Paul the Chief Tech called and told me the position was mine if I was still interested.

I would be living nearby a superb country store and one quarter mile from a river where Precious could net for crabs and seine for fish. Thank You, Lord Jesus!!!

Maggie was in her senior year of high school. She was living with her grandmother, Precious's mother in Ferndale. Maggie would spend most weekends with Precious and I on the Eastern Shore.

Precious had answered an ad by a physician for an assistant in his office as his nurse was retiring. The doctor was very impressed with Precious, then said that he was not going to hire her. Instead, he said, he was going to recommend her for a different position. A friend and patient of his had suffered a serious stroke, was soon to be discharged from extensive rehabilitation, and would require very special care at home. The wife of the patient was the principal at one of the local grammar schools and an exceptional lady. He would call and recommend Precious for the position.

When Precious and Gladys, the wife/principal met, it was like the meeting of lifelong friends. Precious had that effect on people. Precious was to care for Louis, the patient/husband during school hours four days per week. Precious needed to be off work every Friday so that she could be with me every Friday, Saturday, and Sunday. Gladys would arrange for Louis's care on Fridays.

The arrangement worked well until Maggie's graduation, when both she and Precious joined me permanently on the Eastern Shore after Maggie's graduation. The three of us were very happy. Maggie particularly so with her totally reconditioned yellow convertible MGB which we had presented to her as a graduation present.

Precious and I were aware that the Love of Jesus, that had been given to each one of us, was bonding us tighter into the One that we were destined to become. We expressed Our Thanks to You, Dear Jesus, many times each day.

We had spent approximately a year and a half in Maryland and as Paul and I were sitting in the department office, the telephone rang. Paul answered the phone. The call was for me. Paul asked who was calling, then he handed the phone to me. It was the senior physician of a group that staffed a small community hospital in Virginia near where our farm was located. I had done some part-time work with them when we had the farm. The doctor was quickly to the point with the question, "What would it take to have you come and work full-time with us?" This was a "cut to the chase" business conversation. I replied, "Whatever is required." (I had in mind that it would be two and a half years until my forty-eighth birthday and our Five-Year Plan was on schedule.)

We arranged a meeting for the following Saturday at 1 p.m. in the hospital in Virginia. The doctor had located me by calling Mike, our son, to ask how he could contact me. I handed the phone back to Paul. He looked at me and said, "A job offer?" I nodded yes. Paul said, "I have been waiting for that call since the day you came to work here."

I departed from the hospital early to go and inform Precious and Maggie. Precious had a bit of excitement in her voice as she said, "I will be ready to go Saturday." Maggie said with resignation, "Here we go again!!"

As always, Our Dear Lord Jesus was leading us onward. Our prayer was, "May we do the Will of God at all times in all places" and "Yes, Lord!!!"

24

A Return to Virginia

We met the physician in charge and the administrator, whom we both knew well, at the Virginia hospital the following Saturday. We all came to an amicable agreement. We rented a nice brick home on a large lot with many trees with a wide variety of birds located one block from the hospital. At that time, every town in Virginia was designated a bird sanctuary.

We had our mobile home on the Eastern Shore of Maryland moved to a small private park thirty miles west of us and rented it to a young couple that we had known since they were in high school.

Precious and I always looked forward to our weekly afternoon round of golf together. Always only the two of us. It was always a fun day filled with gaiety and laughter. Except at the water hole, which was a nemesis for Precious. It was always an afternoon of love, laughter, and mutual admiration, played on a golf course that had great views of the Blue Ridge Mountains. And Oh! How we Loved each other!!! Mike and his friends often played the course.

My Five-Year Plan was half gone but on schedule. Maggie was an aspiring actress. She had performed very well in high school, with honors. I cautioned her about the many young aspiring Thespians who were having difficulty buying the necessities of survival, including food. She would need a means of self-support while she was honing her craft. Precious and I suggested nursing as a career that would provide that security. I suggested that she work as a trainee nursing assistant before entering any nursing program to see how it appealed to her. She applied for a learning position at the hospital. They would give her a job. After six weeks, she said that she would like to enroll in a school located on the Eastern Shore of Virginia as a student in their LPN program. It was a one-year, hospital-based, live-in program. And by the way, the town had an adult acting group known as the Old Town Players which was formed mostly by people of various professions in the area.

Precious was skeptical. I thought this would be a great lesson in life for Maggie. And she wanted to take her convertible MGB with her! The skepticism of Precious took a giant leap.

We would all need to take a trip of two hundred miles each way to thoroughly check out all aspects of the move.

Maggie enrolled in the class starting in early September and graduating the next Labor Day. She followed us from home to the Eastern Shore in her MGB. The school was a part of the Regional Hospital of the Eastern Shore. It had previously offered a three-year RN program. The teaching staff had all been senior teachers for the three-year program. The graduates of the one-year LPN program were highly recruited by the Army and Navy, both of which had large bases in the Norfolk area. The military recruiters would offer the graduates a rank of sergeant, enroll them into a baccalaureate program at an approved university or college, and upon graduation, the student would be promoted to a junior officer rank up to a captaincy, depending on their performance as a student. In return for the schooling, the graduate was obligated to remain in the service for four or five years. Exceptional students were offered post-graduate schooling.

Maggie was very interested in the program. At graduation, she was second in her class. After graduation, she came home, relaxed for a few weeks, and then went to the Army recruiting office in Charlottesville to enlist.

A reservist staff sergeant was visiting the recruiters. He and Maggie met eye-to-eye and she never served in the military. Affairs of the heart dominated. She joined the nursing staff at Martha Jefferson Hospital in Charlottesville where much later, she became the mother of identical twin boys who weighed a bit over six pounds each.

Time kept ticking by. My forty-eighth birthday would be upon us in a few months. After much thought and prayer, I revealed my new "Five-Year Plan" to Precious. Only this time, the time element would be changeable at a moment's notice and we both were aware and would be ready to accept whatever was in our future.

I would never again work at a full-time job for money or barter.

I went deep within myself and You, Lord Jesus, were there with me. I had to consider all people, things, attachments, everything that was in my life. I had to reduce all down to the least common denominator. I needed to know what was paramount in my life. I was searching my soul with my mind. It was imperative that I know the answer.

After many days and some nights of preoccupation, the answer came to me one evening as Precious and I were relaxing in the living room. The answer hit my mind like a bolt of lightning. There were only two that were paramount in my life. My God and my Precious. All other people and all else was secondary.

Precious and I began making changes. My so-called Five-Year Plan would need much revision or trashed. I notified the owner of the home we were renting that we would be moving in to our mobile home in two months. We notified the couple (who now were parents) who were renting the mobile home on a month-to-month basis that they had two months to relocate as we would be moving into the home in two months. I resigned from every professional or church or any other non-paying position that I held.

We advised our children to get their lives in order as they would be making their own decisions in the future. Precious and I would be moving on. Our children must now begin to take the responsibility for their own actions and inactions. The time had come for each one of them to put on their own mantles of life.

There would no longer be a Five-Year Plan. All plans would be of short duration with possible extensions and all would also be with "The Lord Willing." All of the above went into effect three months prior to my forty-eighth birthday.

We moved into the mobile home. I commuted to work each day. Fall was in the air and we knew that the colder weather would end our weekly golfing outing. All things were changing. But our Love was becoming more "Still" and "Intense."

Six weeks prior to our departure, a Veterinarian

friend whom I had aided in some of his research for the University of Pennsylvania School of Veterinary Medicine, of which he was a graduate, called and asked if I could come to his office. He had something of importance that he wanted to discuss. He suggested that I bring Precious with me. At his office, after greetings, he excused himself and returned holding this six-month-old black miniature poodle. He presented her to me as a token of appreciation for my assisting him in his research which I had done without charge. He said that he would provide care for this beautiful little dog for her entire life, free of charge. We expressed our thanks and informed him of our coming departure. He expressed his dismay. We thanked him for being a friend and departed with the dog. The last thing that Precious and I needed at this time was a dog, no matter how darling.

My resignation was submitted one month before departure to be effective on my forty-eighth birthday.

We had previously arranged to park our mobile home in a privately owned park located in North Myrtle Beach, South Carolina. We would check out the weather there at that time of year. We had called the mobile home transporter that we had used previously, advising date of departure. He said he would be there weather permitting.

Ten days prior to departure, my brother-in-law that married my oldest sister called and stated that she had multiple myeloma. At that time, multiple myeloma was a disease with a low survival rate. Very painful in later stages if bone lesions were prominent. The disease had advanced because it had been misdiagnosed. Calls had been placed to my other two sisters, one living in Kansas City, Missouri, the other near Los Angeles, California. Hotel arrangements were made. We three would arrive at her bedside together.

Discussions with her physicians revealed that her condition would require very aggressive treatment. I knew what that meant. So I asked them to give us twenty-four hours before beginning treatment. They agreed to the delay. She, Irene, requested that I remain at her bedside where I was caressing her aching body. She said that the caressing "felt so very good." She would sleep sporadically. At 10 p.m., a nurse appeared with meds that would induce sleep.

I returned to the hotel to eat a little and to sleep. I arose at 5 a.m., showered, spoke with my sisters, and told them that I would be leaving later that afternoon. I ate lightly and returned to Irene's bedside. She awoke and was happy to see that I was near. She and I had been very close in life and she relied on me. But this time all was out of my control. I tried to reassure her as lovingly as I could that her Faith in the Lord Jesus would be rewarded beyond her dreams. She wanted to live but knew that she would not.

The physicians appeared exactly when my twenty-four hours expired. I prayed with her and kissed her. The doctors were injecting the meds as I took one last look at her.

I walked to the waiting room where her son was waiting with his wife. I gave him the phone numbers in North Myrtle Beach where they could reach me whenever she died.

It was a long, tearful ride back to Virginia where Precious was waiting with tear-filled eyes to greet me. We cried and prayed together as one. And Oh! How we Loved each other!!!

We called Mike and Maggie. We all had dinner together at one of our favorite restaurants. There was much love flowing around with much laughter and remembrances we had lived. It was a family fun evening. We kissed, embraced, and loved as we all said our goodbyes and best wishes. Precious and I were two happy parents.

My day of resignation was a day filled with handshakes, hugs, and thanks and best wishes between friends and associates. Our mobile home transporter called and said that he would be two days late because of adverse weather. We relaxed, rested, and enjoyed our new young dog, Jodie.

Buddy arrived to transport the mobile home. We got a late start and had to stop at a motel/restaurant place because of darkness. Mobile homes are not permitted on highways in low light conditions. We would arrive at North Myrtle Beach, South Carolina, the following afternoon.

It did not take us long to determine that the Myrtle Beach area was not for us during the winter months.

While in the area we took Jodie to a veterinarian to be spayed. She did not survive the anesthesia.

We secured the mobile home with the furnace "on" for adequate heating, gave a key to the park owner for emergencies, along with phone numbers to call if need be. We paid the storage fee for another month, packed some clothing, and headed to Florida for warmer weather.

25

Precious and Seashells

Precious was fascinated by the structure and coloring of seashells. She possessed many books and articles about shells and shelling. I had always been a nature lover and fishing was getting close to nature for me. The adage "give a person a fish and they will eat for a day; teach a person how to fish and they can eat for a lifetime" was one that I subscribed to.

Precious's love of shell collecting and my love of fishing fit together like hand in glove. We shelled and fished together along the Atlantic Coast from Delaware to Key West, Florida. Along the way we found many seafood restaurants that served well-prepared fresh seafood. Many were located where party boats operated and then sold their "catch of the day" to the restaurants upon arrival after a day of fishing.

Shelling is generally most productive in areas where there are turbulent waters. A few of these waters are at the Outer Banks of North Carolina (also known as "the Graveyard of the Atlantic"), the Florida Keys, and the coast along the Gulf of Mexico after hurricane season.

Once on a trip to the Outer Banks, Precious met a lady that was a "sheller" who told Precious about a scallop processing plant located on one of the islands. Precious made sure that I could find that plant early the next morning before sunrise. They used a conveyor belt that transported the empty scallop shells (plus many other species that lived at the same depth but were not harvested) outdoors to the rear of the plant where they formed a large pile. The shells would later be ground up to be used as fertilizer. Precious had me use our small shovel to move the shells as she held and examined ones of interest. Before long, the sun began to shine on the shell pile. The pile began to produce a strong stench. An older male worker appeared at the pile. I said to him, "I would guess that this pile attracts many rats after dark each night." He replied, "Yes sir, very large rats." When Precious heard what the man said, she began a rapid in place dance. The man and I applauded and asked for an encore, to which Precious replied, "Let's get out of here now!" And then she laughed as we entered our truck.

As all serious "shellers" knew in the 1970s, whenever there was a strong hurricane in the Eastern Gulf of Mexico during the hurricane season, there is only one place to go shelling the following December. And that place was Sanibel Island, located off the West Coast of Florida not far from Fort Myers.

A swath of live animals in perfect or near perfect shells stacked a foot or so high and five feet wide. Precious was in sheller's paradise. She was collecting only perfect specimens for me to remove the live animals without damaging the shells. Yes, Precious, anything for you!

Once on a trip down to the Florida Keys, Precious found a fourteen and a half inch long horse conch which is the official state shell of the State of Florida. She was very fond and proud of her find as it was a perfect specimen. To celebrate the occasion, we ate some conch chowder after arriving in Key West. We followed the conch chowder with some Key Lime Pie. And Oh! How I Loved her!!!

Upon arrival back home near Orlando, while admiring her conch specimen, I told her that I also possessed a horse conch specimen. Her eyes sparkled with surprise as I returned to the room to show her a one inch long baby horse conch shell. I told her that I had been secretly amassing a collection of perfect baby seashells. I showed her my collection of miniature shells each wrapped with cotton for protection. Precious was surprised and thrilled as I gave her the collection. And Oh! How I Loved her!!!

I asked her what she was going to do with all of those collected shells. She said she was going to display her best ones and give the others to relatives and friends.

Soon afterwards, we took a ride to an arts and crafts store where Precious purchased six shadow boxes of which three were the same size. She also purchased several containers of mounting glue.

She pre-positioned the shells in the boxes and then had me mount the shells. Three boxes were arranged for display on our living room wall and the others given away. They were truly works of art done by the mind of a true artist, my Precious!

Another shell that she owned was a chambered nautilus. It was of very good size with excellent coloring. She admired the beauty and the story of the life cycle and feeding process and habitat of that species. Precious's love of shells stayed throughout her lifetime.

In our bathroom, in our daughter's home, this day, hangs a shower curtain with the very detailed imprints of, you guessed it, seashells of many species.

The loves of Precious, no matter the object, more times than not, lasted a lifetime. Most of her Love was deep seated and long lasting.

26

Granny and Her Progeny

Did I mention children? Yes, we had two, one boy and one girl. Grandchildren: four. Three boys, of which two are identical twins, and one girl. Great grandchildren: ten. Six boys, of which two are twins, and four girls. I am the only one who uses the name Precious. All others call her Mom, Momma, or Granny. All love her deeply as she loves them. When speaking about her when she was not present, they at times would refer to her as Pop's Precious. Never Precious alone directed at her.

One of our treasured gifts in life is that our son, Michael, and our three grandsons Matthew,

Christopher, and Nathan are all loving, caring husbands and fathers. A True Blessing from Our Dear Lord Jesus, of which there have been many! We Thank You, Lord! We Thank You!!!

27

From Many Nations, Peoples, and Tongues

And then there were the thousands upon thousands of human beings that Our Dear Lord Jesus brought into our lives. From all continents except Antarctica. From most, but not all, countries. We managed to communicate with all in some way or another. We loved them all. They all, without exception, loved Precious. Why? Because she always loved them first. My "angel" in human flesh! However, there were rare occasions when we did not agree with the words and actions of a few. Most were fellow country persons of the United States.

Only by the Love and Grace of our Dear Lord Jesus have we been privileged to share a Love and

Life together. We may not have experienced it all, but we have shared a large part of it, probably more than most.

What a Love! What a Life! Through it all, You were there with us, Lord Jesus, and most of the time we were aware of Your Presence, and we Thank You!!! Thank You!!! Our Hymn of Praise and Thanksgiving is Eternal!!!

And now, Lord Jesus, I ask that You give me the Strength of Mind and Body and Soul to write the final chapters of this Love Story. To You O Lord, I lift up my Soul!

28

A Lifetime of Togetherness

From the moment Precious and I first sat and talked while sitting in that backyard gazebo and throughout our lifetime together, we were content to be alone with each other. The exception was in 1969 when disposing of the farm. From 1969 on, if we were separated for any length of time, on rare occasions, it would be heart wrenching for us. We truly had become One. We would finish each other's sentences. I would start to sing a song, she would say, "I was just thinking about that song." It was uncanny. We were always on the same "wavelength."

Whenever we were walking any distances, short or long, we held hands. If both of my hands were full of anything, she would hold onto my shirt, sweater, or jacket. We walked hand in hand everywhere, in church, down sidewalks, on beaches, in parks, from car to shops, in shopping centers. And while sitting together at home and momentarily while eating.

I massaged or caressed her body sometime every day. She loved massage and caresses. Precious and I believed that touch was a great relaxer and healer and sleep inducer. Touch, we believed, was one great sense that should be used often daily. We caressed our children and our grandchildren from infancy to adulthood. I caressed my fifty-two year old sister as she lay dying. You can "touch" deeply by only using your eyes.

On several occasions, as we were walking or standing hand in hand, strangers would ask for our permission to photograph us hand in hand. One lady in Walmart, a total stranger, turned and said, "Watching you two just made my day. Thank you!" I replied, "Thank Jesus." We knew that It was Your Love that You had implanted within us that we were giving away to any and all who chose to receive it. We Thank and we Praise You, Lord Jesus!" Total strangers would walk up to us as we were walking and say, "I don't know who you are, but will you give me your autograph?" We complied with every request because all experiences were very humbling for us.

For fifty years, Precious and I considered ourselves as lowly servants who were blessed to be seed-planters. The only seeds we planted were seeds of Love. We planted seed by every means available to us. We planted seeds from the Atlantic to the Pacific. We were not preachers, except on very rare occasions. We were planters. We knew within our hearts that some seed fell on rocky ground and did not sprout. Some fell on sandy soil, sprouted, but later died. Some seed was planted on fertile soil, took root, sprouted and grew to produce much grain.

We did not cultivate except on rare occasions. Cultivating was to be done by others. The entire harvest belongs to our Heavenly Father as Presented to Him by His Son, Our Lord and Savior, Jesus, who is the Christ. To Him Be All Honor, Glory, Praise, and Thanksgiving Now and Forever. Amen!!! Amen!!!

To all who read or hear this true story of two

ordinary people who had been filled with Love, we pray that our Dear Lord Jesus will touch each of you with The Fire of His Love and may He Bless you with Peace of Mind and Peace of Soul Now and Forever. And all say with one voice Amen!!! Amen!!!

29

Seventy-Seven (77) Years, Two Months Later

My Dear Lord and Savior Jesus!!! As I continue writing, I will be singing my song of Praise and Thanksgiving to You for all that You have given me. I am so humbled by Your continuing Presence because I am so undeserving of Your Consuming Love. We Praise You! Let all of the people, everywhere, Praise You!!!

As I write this, my Precious is fourteen days from beginning her ninety-third year of life. In a couple of months, I may be entering my ninety-fourth year. In a little more than a month, we may celebrate our seventy-third year of marriage. We are aware, of course, that we are not guaranteed the remainder of today. God's Will be done in all things, at all times.

What a Love Affair we have shared. Almost unbelievable. So much Loving and Living that it could be enough material for the writing of many books. However, the only book that we desire and pray that our names are written in is the Lamb's Book of Life!!! In the Bible, Philippians 4:3, Revelations 3:5, 13:8 and 21:27.

Precious and I always believed that Life is given to us for living. Therefore, we lived It to the fullest. And then some more. War and Peace, Happiness and Heartache, Life-Threatening Illnesses and Good Health, Togetherness and Separation, Honors and Ridicule. We have shared having much and conversely, have shared having little. Such as fine gourmet dining, then bologna sandwiches and everything in between. We have shed blood, sweat, and tears in Maryland, Pennsylvania, West Virginia, Virginia, North Carolina, Florida, Colorado, New Mexico, Arizona, and Texas. We have traveled and walked hand in hand along areas of the Atlantic from New Jersey to Key West, areas of the Gulf of

Mexico from Chokoloskee to Pensacola, Florida and areas from Galveston to Corpus Christi, Texas. We have traveled and walked along areas of the Pacific Ocean from San Diego to San Francisco. Hand in hand we have traveled and walked the Atlantic Coastal Plain, the Piedmont, the Appalachian Mountains, the Midwest, The Great Plains, the Rocky Mountains, the Desert Southwest, the High Plains, the High Sierras. We have traveled and walked from below sea level to above fourteen thousand foot elevation until restricted by advancing age.

We have Lived and Loved in large cities, small cities, large towns, small towns, in the country, on a farm. We have lived in the desert, on the high plains, on a ranch, along rivers, lakes, and at the seashore. And Oh! How I Loved her!

We have traveled by automobile, trains, planes, boats, and ships. By bus, street car, taxi, limousine. We have owned nine recreational vehicles of all shapes and sizes. We owned a boat for fishing and water sport.

Did I mention that Precious really enjoyed white water rafting on Wild and Scenic Rivers?

And drawing sketches of everywhere we traveled and reading books, collecting seashells, pine cones, wild flowers, rocks and gems, leaves from any and all trees, to press in the pages of her books. And dried flowers and weeds for the centerpiece of our Thanksgiving table. So artistic, so talented, so lovable, and so natural with it all.

30

All Things Are Passing, and This Also Shall Pass

With all of the love and strength that I now possess, I must write the following:

During the past three years, my Precious, who lost most of her eyesight nineteen years ago and has difficulty with hearing, has been waging a battle with cancer that is now raging throughout her body.

Following the biopsy of the initial tumor in her right breast, many examinations and much testing was performed in an attempt to detect additional growth and the ability of her heart to tolerate the proposed surgery.

Upon receipt of the comprehensive pathology report that stated there were four different types of cancer cells within that one tumor and a diagnosis of metaplastic breast cancer, and after perusing the latest international literature and consultations with cardiologists, anesthesiologists, and surgeons, the prognosis was deemed: poor.

Precious was and is heroic throughout all thus far. She has been totally involved in all her medical care and the final decision on her care after consultation and discussion is made by her. She desired quality of life over and above quantity of life. I respected her decision and gave her one hundred percent support and I requested that all others do likewise, including her physicians. She opted for surgery, followed only by palliative care.

Precious has said goodbye to her oncology team, and for the past six months, has been under hospice care here at the home of our daughter, Maggie. Our son Michael speaks with her daily from his home in Virginia and visited her monthly until she requested that he visit less frequently because of his health. That is my Precious, always concerned about others rather than herself. She who nursed and always gave care and compassion to others is now being nursed and cared for by others.

All that I ask of You, Lord Jesus, is that You give me the strength and ability to continue caring for her 24/7. I will care for her until one or both of us takes our last breath.

31

The Last Words of Precious

Precious and I, all of our married life, with only a few exceptions because of job requirements, would go to bed each night together, at the same time. We had "pillow talk" every night that we were together for over seventy-three years.

Whenever I sensed that Precious was near going off to sleep, as music was always playing softly, I would say to her, "Nighty night, my Precious, God bless you, I love you, Precious."

Then she would say to me, "Nighty night, Poppy, God bless you, I love you" as she fell into sleep.

Three nights before she died, I said to her, as I sensed she was getting ready to nod off, "Nighty night, my Precious, God bless you, I love you, Precious."

In her voice weakened by suffering, she replied "Nighty night, Poppy, God bless you, I love you—with all my heart." She went off to sleep.

And You were there, Sweet Jesus, as I cried myself to sleep.

My Precious never spoke again.

All who know us know that my Precious and I will burn with a Love for each other that will not end with death.

Our Love is from God!
Because God is Love!!!

I John 4:8, 4:16.

Deo Gratias!!!

And now, Lord Jesus, I end this very limited short story of the Love and Life that you bestowed on my Precious and me as I began it. Praising and Thanking You, my Lord and my God. You have been with us throughout our journey. Most of the time, we were consciously aware of Your Presence. Conversely, we were very aware at times that our thoughts, words, and actions were not pleasing to You. We are only "little children" Dear Lord, always in need of Your Love and Guidance.

Lord, as we transition from this life to Life Everlasting, we look forward with joyful hope to sharing our Love with All, in All, within Your Love. As our Hymn of Praise and Thanksgiving reverberates throughout the Cosmos Forever and Ever. Amen! Amen!!!

And all who read or hear this story say Amen!!!

32

An Angel, My Precious, Returns to Heaven

I t was on the bright Sunday morning of February 17, 2019 at 9:10 a.m. that Our Dear Lord Jesus came and held his "angel," my Precious, by the hand and led her to be with Him and with the Angels and Saints and the Multitude of Heavenly Hosts through Eternity!!!

The Lord gave and the Lord has taken away. Blessed be the Name of the Lord Now and Forever. Amen!!! Amen!!!

My grief was overwhelming! I had difficulty breathing. I could not see well because of the flow of tears.

Her mouth was open.

I held her chin and gently closed her mouth. It remained closed.

I held her head with both hands and as softly and as gently as I could, I kissed my Precious the same way I had given her her first kiss seventy-eight years earlier when she was fourteen years of age.

I kissed her forehead.

And then something happened that I had never witnessed previously.

I had been witness to many as they were dying or at their actual deaths in many places. In battlefields, ERs, highways, hospitals, and homes.

Soon after I kissed her, her lips became visibly sealed.

Instantly, I checked the pupils of her eyes and all of her vital signs. All were "flat-lined."

My Precious had clinically expired.

With my phone, I took a picture of her with her lips sealed. It was then that I knew why her lips were sealed.

You, Sweet Jesus, were there with us and it was You who had sealed her lips.

As my Precious lay lifeless with Maggie and Sherry, her favorite nurse, nearby ...

with two morticians waiting to remove
her lifeless, cancer-ridden body ...
with tears flowing ...
I removed her socks ...
bathed both of her feet with my tears ...
and then I kissed each foot three times.

And Oh! How I Love her!!!
And Oh! How I will always Love her!!!

To You, Sweet Jesus,
I lift up my Precious!!!
To You, Sweet Jesus, I lift up my Soul!!!

About the Author

A graduate of The Johns Hopkins School of Radiologic Technology.

A Senior Engineering Technician. A General Contractor. A Technical Director. A salesman. And a Planter.

Printed in the United States
By Bookmasters